Flying Foxes

by Grace Hansen

SPOOKY ANIMALS

Abdo Kids Jumbo is an Imprint of Abdo Kids
abdobooks.com

abdobooks.com

Published by Abdo Kids, a division of ABDO, P.O. Box 398166, Minneapolis, Minnesota 55439.
Copyright © 2021 by Abdo Consulting Group, Inc. International copyrights reserved in all countries.
No part of this book may be reproduced in any form without written permission from the publisher.
Abdo Kids Jumbo™ is a trademark and logo of Abdo Kids.

Printed in the United States of America, North Mankato, Minnesota.

052020

092020

Photo Credits: Alamy, iStock, Shutterstock

Production Contributors: Teddy Borth, Jennie Forsberg, Grace Hansen
Design Contributors: Dorothy Toth, Pakou Moua

Library of Congress Control Number: 2019956566
Publisher's Cataloging-in-Publication Data

Names: Hansen, Grace, author.

Title: Flying foxes / by Grace Hansen

Description: Minneapolis, Minnesota : Abdo Kids, 2021 | Series: Spooky animals | Includes online resources
and index.

Identifiers: ISBN 9781098202491 (lib. bdg.) | ISBN 9781098203474 (ebook) | ISBN 9781098203962
(Read-to-Me ebook)

Subjects: LCSH: Flying foxes--Juvenile literature. | Fox bats--Juvenile literature. | Bats--Juvenile literature.
| Nocturnal animals--Behavior--Juvenile literature.

Classification: DDC 596.018--dc23

Table of Contents

Flying Foxes

Flying foxes live in warm areas with forests. They can be found in places like Indonesia, Madagascar, and Australia.

Indonesia

Madagascar   Australia

5

A flying fox is actually a bat. It is called a fox because its head looks like a fox's. It has a pointed nose, large eyes, and short, upright ears.

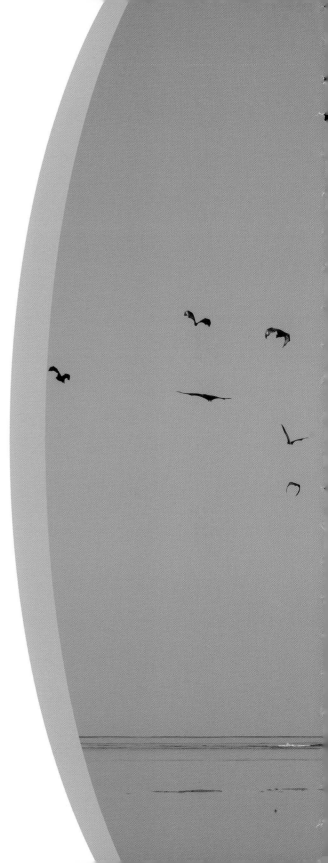

There are more than 60 flying fox **species**. Some are larger than others.

Larger kinds of flying foxes have giant **wingspans**. Their wingspans can measure more than 4 feet (1.2 m)!

11

While flying foxes are big, they don't weigh much. Most weigh just 3 pounds (1.4 kg).

Their light weight and large wings help them fly. Bats are the only **mammals** that can **sustain** flight.

Food

Flying foxes are fruit bats.

This means they eat fruit.

But their favorite foods are

flowers and nectar.

16

17

Roosting

Flying foxes **roost** together in groups. Their large toes grip onto tree branches. They hang upside down.

18

19

Baby Flying Foxes

Baby flying foxes cling to their mothers. Their mothers carry them for 4 to 5 weeks. After that, the babies are too heavy. At around 12 weeks, young flying foxes can fly and eat on their own.

Index

Abdo Kids ONLINE
FREE! ONLINE MULTIMEDIA RESOURCES

Visit **abdokids.com** to access crafts, games, videos, and more!

Use Abdo Kids code

SFK2491

or scan this QR code!